The Book o

or "Mekya Self

By Ray Tenn

with Cartoons by Jim Lyndon

Random Thoughts on the Dialect and Accent of Britain's Premier City (Brumslang) with a Glossary of the Most Common Expressions plus Brumodes, Brumverse and Brumericks with a little More Serious Verse

Contents

Published by

Westwood Press Publications

44 Boldmere Road, Sutton Coldfield, West Midlands

021-354 5913

Ray Tennant was born in Birmingham and has lived here all his life. Educated at Saltley Grammar School and St. Peter's College, Saltley, he has taught in Birmingham Junior and Secondary Schools and was until recently Deputy Head Teacher at The Arden School, Bordesley Green.

He has been interested in dialects and accents for many years and confesses to having acquired several of the "Brumslang" expressions in this book during his teaching career.

His poetry has been broadcast and some has been published in the *Birmingham Post* and *Country Quest*. He has also published several articles on educational matters and the local dialect in the press.

For B.J.T. (Old Friend)

© Copyright 1982 by Westwood Press
First Edition December 1982
2nd Impression December 1982
3rd Impression February 1983

Printed and published by The Westwood Press, Print Shop, 44 Boldmere Road, Sutton Coldfield, West Midlands. Produced by photo offset, text phototypeset in Rockwell.

Foreword

With one or two notable exceptions, such as Beryl Reid and more recently Don Maclean and Jasper Carrott, the dialect of Birmingham has been rather neglected in the entertainment field and certainly considered rather "non-U" in social circles. Compared to the popularisation of Scouse since Beatlemania and Geordie since that "Boat Came In", the warm country sound of Pam Ayres and the ever present Cockney tones, it is my belief that Brummy has been given something of a raw deal.

Over the past few years, therefore, I have been making a fairly intensive study of my native city's accent and attempting to put it down phonetically for the benefit of foreigners — meaning, of course, anyone north of Sutton Coldfield, south of Rubery, west of Wolverhampton and east of Solihull.

It is interesting to note that whilst many budding future Yarwoods fancy themselves at a bit of Yorkshire or Lancashire, Welsh or Gloucestershire, and can make a reasonable go with these dialects, I have not found many people who can really get a genuine Brummy sound. This may well be because there has been no great movement in the Pop World or so successful a TV series as "When the Boat Comes In", which has emphasised the Brummy accent. Consequently the general public has not been exposed to it at any great length — and perhaps some of them are grateful for that!

A geographical study of the actual placement of Brummie is very interesting to undertake, if you are one of those people, like me, who finds the actual sounds of voices fascinating. If one moves, for example, out towards Nuneaton one notices a gradual change from Brummie into a Warwickshire sound. Similarly, as you move south of Rubery the sound becomes more rural. Moving North it takes on a

Dedicated to awl the

citizens of Brumijum

from the Lord Mare

to the mowst

'umble ritepiyer.

harsher sound as you enter Staffordshire and to the West, of course, is that other great dialect of the Midlands, Black Country, which is almost another language.

What is really intriguing, though, is how did it start, where did it start — even why did it start and how did it congeal into that singularly Brummy sound? Oider now ar kid but it really meksya think, doanit?

However, new students should study the glossary carefully and if they follow the phonetics faithfully, they should be able to pass themselves off as almost the genuine article in most city bus queues, railway stations, pubs and other places of assembly.

To test their skills I have included a few passages and some light verse for practice, not all written entirely in Brumslang since too much phonetic writing sometimes leads to confusion.

Finally, having been a native of Birmingham all of my life, I have sometimes been saddened to see some of its distinguished landmarks disappear, and so I have included a few poems of a more serious and nostalgic nature as well as a couple which comment on city life generally.

I can only conclude by emphasising my affection for the place which "as bin me um fer sow many yairs."

Ray Tennant

"Arffa Bitta"

A Glossary of Brumslang

acha
atcha   Various forms of greeting derived from the
adoo   basic "How do you do?"
arjudoo

affpass   The half hour on the clock, e.g. in answer to
                   "stoim?" (q.v.)
affpast   "Affpasten" (10.30), "Affpastate" (8.30).

allow?   Exclamatory question usually meaning "What
                   matter did you wish to discuss with me?" Also
                   used to open telephone conversations.

acawss   Most definitely, decidedly. E.g. "Acawss oil
                   gew if yow say so."

annawl   Not a small tool used by shoemakers but an
                   expression meaning "as well", or "also".
                   E.g. "'e as anawl" : he has as well
                   or "'e did anawl" : he did, as well.

ar   The affirmative "Yes" in answer to a question.
                   Also "our" as in "ar kid", meaning frequently
                   "my younger brother" or often simply and con
                   solingly "my friend".

arffa   Half an imperial pint as in "arffa bitta" or "arffa
                   moild" — "half of bitter" or "half of mild".
                   Nothing to do with the King and the Round
                   Table.

"Carntcha stop the bab croin? Geris windup."

arffabar

arffadolla

Now somewhat archaic and only occasionally used since decimalisation, meaning respectively the old ten shilling note and half a crown.

arnarff

A form of emphasis, e.g. "They arnarff daft", meaning "They are indeed very silly".

avya?

The question "Do you possess?", e.g. "Avya gorra pen?" — "Do you possess a pen?". Or another form of emphasis as in "Yow int, avya?" meaning "Have you really?"

awlwiz

On every occasion. Never missing, as in "'e's awlwiz doin' that".

awroit

Meaning that's OK or all right.

ax
axed
ast

All forms of questioning, e.g. "Oi axed (ast) 'im if oi could gew". Meaning "I requested permission to leave".

bab

A baby or very often *the* baby as in "Carntcha (q.v.) stop the bab croin'? Geriz windup".

baird

The feminine of the human species.

blart

To cry or weep.

blastid

A slightly milder form of expletive than "bloody".

bloimy
bludyell

Expressions of surprise, amazement or sometimes annoyance, e.g. Wot the bludyell's up with you?"

A buzz and a boozer

blowk	The masculine of the human species.
boozer	An inn or hostelry.
borrow me	Frequently used by school children meaning ''lend me'', e.g. ''Sucunnya borrow me a pen?'' — ''Please sir will you lend me a pen?''
Brumijum	Where it awl startid!
buzz	A public service vehicle — well-known form of transport in Brumijum. Plural is ''buzziz''.
caff	A place of refreshment, usually with ''Space Invaders'' and other machines.
carntcha?	Can you not? Are you not able? — ''Carntcha turn that woiliss (q.v.) down? It's definin' me.
cawss	See acawss
copolte	Take a firm grip, catch this or grab a hold. As in the well-known saying ''copolte ov this amma and nile an' wen oi nod mi 'ed, 'it it''.
croikey	A mild expression of surprise which might follow the well-known saying above!
cummoffit	I simply do not believe you. You must be joking.
cut	Well-known expression for a canal, thus: ''Oimagunna gew up the cut'' could mean ''I am going for a walk beside, a voyage on, or simply a journey to the canal.

"Copolte ov this amma and nile an' when oi nod mi
'ed, 'it it."

daint

dainya
daintcha

Variations on "did not", thus: "Daintcha loik yer dinna?" (q.v.) meaning "Was the lunch which I cooked for you not to your liking?"

deesul

A type of train operating usually on local routes.

dinna

A mid-day meal. (N.B. in Brum this is never called "lunch", which is a mid-morning snack especially for school children. Lunch is also a dinna eaten by posh people.

doanit?

(Must have a drawn out, lazy vowel sound). Means "Does it not?" E.g. "Doanit mekya (q.v.) sick!"

dyow
or
jow

"Do you" as in "Dyownow wot toim it is?" meaning usually "Do you realise how late it is?" Also "Dyow moind?", meaning usually "Do not refer to me in that way".

earowl

The orifice which is the centre of auditory perception. Of a person who is hard of hearing one sometimes says "Stoim yow washed yer earowls out". Also used to mean currying favour, as in "Stop yer earowlin". Hence an "Earowler" (Sycophant).

ee-a!

Exclamation for "here!", usually meaning "Watch it or I'll thump you one" as a warning.

er

Quite frequently simply "she", as in "er nose", meaning "she is perfectly well aware of this fact".

ern

Belonging to her, e.g. "It's ern," meaning "This is her property".

eeyar

"Here you are", meaning "I am proposing to give this to you".

forus

"For me", as in "Willya gew forus?", meaning "Will you go on this errand for me?" or "Will you deliver this message for me?"

fuddeffinit

Definitely or certainly, e.g. "I will certainly meet you at 8.30 tomorrow morning" would be "Oil seeya at affpasstate tomorra mawnin fuddeffinit".

gardin

A place for growing flowers and vegetables. Most owziz in Brum have a "backun" and a "fruntun".

garridge

A place for storing and for servicing vehicles (including buzziz).

gear
gearsa
geyussa

Variations on donating. E.g. "Gear sit ear" — — "Please give it to me". "Gearsa sung" — Please sing to me". "Geyussa gew" — "May I have a turn?"

gerroff

Can be used for a variety of situations, e.g. "Excuse me but you are standing on my foot" or "You have reached the end of your journey on this bus" or "You must be fooling. I simply do not believe you".

gerrout
gerraway

Other exclamations meaning "Really" or "You do surprise me". The first of these is also used by angry school teachers who have had enough or a recalcitrant class or pupil. It then means "Would you please leave the room?".

gew

Quite simply "go" — thus the present participle "gewin", meaning "going". "Oima gewin um" means "I intend to return to my place of residence".

gob

The mouth and vocal organs. So "Please be quiet" would be "Shut ya gob".

gorra

Do you own or possess? Thus "Gorra fag mite?" is "Excuse me, my friend, but have you a cigarette to spare?"

guvamint

The political party which has gained the most votes and sits in the "Owziz of Parlimint".

guz

Simply "goes" as in "It guz loik a bom", meaning usually "My vehicle is running very well". (Guzunda is a very ancient name for a chamber pot but I do not think it is necessarily of Brumijum origin).

guzzon

Frequently applied to someone who talks a great deal, e.g. "The wie 'e guzzon!"

holt

Not to be confused with a soldier's order to stop smartly, this is usually found in the expression "Get holt of" meaning "to obtain".

inarff

See "arnarff".

"Mekya Selfa Tum"

incha??   "Are you not?" as in "Incha gewin out?" meaning "Are you not going out?" Also "have you not?" — "Incha gorra pen?"

int   Usually combined in phrases such as "Intit?" (not a common garden bird) meaning "Is it not?"

intergunna   I do not wish or intend to co-operate. (Not the man in charge of armaments half-way down the fuselage of a Flying Fortress).

int struck   Not very impressed. Thus "Oi doan care if Shikespeer writ it or not, oi int struck", meaning "Even though its author was the Bard of Avon, it does not impress me".

isn   Belonging to him. E.g. "It's isn", — "It belongs to him".

jawanna   "Would you like or care for —?" so, "Jawanna cuppa tea an' an am sanwich?" could be "Would you care for some light refreshment?"

julyka   Again "would you like or care for —?" Thus "Julyka cuppa tea, mite, woil yer witing?" means "Would you care for some liquid refreshment during this interval?"

kid   Usually younger brother but see "arkid".

kiddin'   Fooling, deceiving, e.g. "a yow kiddin'?" — "Are you fooling me?"

17

moin Belonging to me.

mekya Make your. Useful in a greeting as in "Mekya selfa tum" — Make yourself at home, i.e. please feel free to use the whole house.

meksya It makes you, as in "Meksya sik, doan it?" meaning "It really is most distressing or upsetting".

mi (Short vowel) meaning "my", as in "Mi dinna" — my mid-day meal.

nunk Nothing, e.g. "Wunt costya nunk", meaning "it is free".

odge Stomach, as in "Stuffin yer odge", which means having a good meal. There is a place in Brum called "Odge Ill Common" which must originally have been the name of a normal mild complaint caused by over indulgence.

oi Singular pronoun, first person "I". Also a way of calling attention to someone, as in "Oi yow — push off!" meaning "Would you mind leaving as soon as possible?"

oidernow I do not know. This is a standard reply to such questions as "oozizit?" (q.v.)

oil Not a lubricant. Singular pronoun "I" followed by "will" or "shall", e.g. "Oil puncher ed (q.v.) if yow doant push off!" meaning "Drastic measures may ensue if you refuse to go".

THE OWLMAN ACAWS

AN THISIS MOI OWLGEL!

oimagunna   I am going to — as in "Awroit mite, oimagunna gew" in reply to request above.

oozizit?   To whom does this item belong?

owlgel   My wife
owlman   My husband

owziz   Places of residence, e.g. cownsil owziz, proivit owziz, freeowld owziz etc. Also public owziz and, as listed above, the Owziz of Parliamint.

owsyerfatha Coy and now somewhat outdated expression for W.C.

pleas to mee cha Not a Latin-American dance but a useful introductory greeting, e.g. in reply to "This is the owlgel or owlman" meaning "I am delighted to make your acquaintance".

plaiziz Areas to visit or positions gained in examinations or athletic competitions.

ploit Well brought up, cultivated and attentive to others.

poil A stack or a large number of things placed on top of one another as in the well-known expression "Oiv gorra poilamoiloi" meaning "have a great deal of work to do".

pointer Not a breed of dog but one imperial pint as in "Pointa Bitta" or "Pointer Moild" — measures of refreshing liquids.

praps Perhaps, maybe.

puncher ed Frequently used when assuming an aggressive posture, e.g. "Oil puncher ed it yow doan't wachit". Meaning "I shall be obliged to administer a blow to your face if you are not more circumspect".

Reuters   Not a News Agency as popularly supposed but a mid-spelling of roiters — ie. "blowks wot roit buks".

roit   Opposite of left, or currently an expression inserted frequently when outlining an argument, e.g. "Oil tellya wor 'appened (Roit). There woz this blowk (Roit) etc. etc. Also used emphatically it can be used as an invitation for a punch up as in "Roit! Now yow've ast for it!"

rung   Opposite of roit, e.g. "'ers done it rung," meaning "She has not acted correctly".

saffta   After I have eaten my lunch, or more likely, mi dinna. i.e. this afternoon.

sanwich   Two pieces of bread with some delicacy in between, e.g. am sanwich, jam sanwich.

sinky   Sometimes used for "I think he" as in "Sinky bloody az anawl," meaning "I should jolly well think he has, too!"

shurrup   Please be quiet! — other variations are "beltup" or more archaically "wrapup".

shutya   Usually combined with "gob" or more vehemently "bleednole", meaning "I do not wish you to continue talking. I have heard enough".

Puncher ed: "Oil puncher 'ed if yow doan't wachit."

smarra?	"What is troubling you?" or "Is there anything amiss?"
sow	Not a female pig — simply the adverb and conjunction "so".
spouse sow	I suppose that must be the case.
sroit	It is correct, as in "Sroit, thou, intit?" meaning "Am I not correct in my statement?" Frequently used in arguments to underline a point.
stickit	Quite simply "Thank you very much but I do not require this article any longer".
stoim?	What hour of the clock is it?
sucunna **sucunnya**	Respectively "Please Sir, may I?" and "Please Sir, will you?" E.g. "Sucunna gew toilit?" means "Please Sir, may I go to relieve myself?" and "Sucunnya gearsa pen?" means "Please Sir, will you give me a pen?"
summut	Simply, something — as in "Is summut up?" meaning "Is something bothering you?"
sup?	Similar to "smarra?"
Sue Ridge	(Not a charmer like Nationwide's Sue Lawley or Sue Cooke unfortunately). An expression for muck which has to be treated at a Sue Ridge Farm.

tairminus   The end of a buzz root.

tekya   Take your — useful expression for a greeting, e.g. "Tekya-cowt-off" — "Please remove your outer garment," or even "Tekyaratoff" (not a Soviet agent).

therewuz   A common introduction to a story, e.g. "Therewuz this blowksy", meaning roughly "Once upon a time there was a man, see?"

tickit   A small paper receipt given for payment of a fare (not to be confused with "stickit").

tie   A child's plaything.

tinarff   It most certainly has or is, e.g. "Tinarff ot this mawnin' ", meaning "The temperature this morning is very high".

toilits   Places for ablutions or more basic natural functions (particularly after affpassten!)

trar   Most common expression for "Goodbye".

ussis
ussid   Variations of "I said" as in "Sow ussis ter this blowk", meaning "So I informed this gentleman"

voyal   Distinctly unpleasant, as in "That suit yaw

wearin' looks voyal", meaning "I do not approve of your taste in clothes".

wa "I beg your pardon?" or "Excuse me, but I did not quite hear what you said".

wairthy ell "Where the hell" as in "Wairthy ell dya think yaw gewin?", which means, for example, "Sorry but this is a one-way street".

wornt Was not — as in "Wornt me, mite," meaning "I am not guilty, officer".

windas Frames with glass in which allow "loit" into a room.

woiliss A radio receiver.
worrow Another form of greeting. See acha etc.

writ Not a legal term but one frequently used instead of "written" or "wrote", especially by schoolchildren, e.g. "Mi Mom's writ ya a note suh" or "Oiv just writ a story".

wuncha "Wuncha gearsa gew?" meaning "Will you not let me have my turn?"

wunt Will not, or will you not?

wuzzagunna "I did intend to" or "I was intending to —" So, for example: "It was my intention to travel today but I shall not go until tomorrow. Then I shall most certainly go," would be: "Oi wuzzagunna gew today but oi intergunna gew till tomorra —

"Oi wuzzagunna gew today but oi intagunna gew till tomorra — then oi amagunna gew fuddeffinit."

then oi amagunna gew — fuddeffinit." (which is a good sentence for practising your consonants!"

yawn

Belonging to you, as in "Is thisn yawn? — No, its isn," meaning "Does this belong to you? No, it belongs to him".

yuwa?

Another expression for "I beg your pardon?" (See "wa").

Some well-known Districks and Plaiziz
of Istoricul Intrest

Aglee Wair thairs an awl an a big ill.

Airdintun Wair thairs the owldist pub called "The Lad in the Line" wot dates from 1386 an woz used by the Rown Deads an Cava Leers jurin the Sivul Wore.

Amstid Wair the cowl moin is.

Anns Wuth Wair Mathyou Bowlton, Jimes Wot an awl them utha clevva blowks startid thair Sow-ow wairks.

Arbun Wair some ov the posher blowks live.

Aston Wair thairs an awl with a mewseeyum, a yooni-vairsity, Ansull's Broory, a cross an the Villa oov wun the cup more toims than ennywun else — so thair!

Bairchfield Oam ov the arrias.

Bornvil wair they mek the choclit.
Broily Ill Wair the Emeebee is.

Canon Ill Nowtid for its luvlee park (It awlsow means the vicca's mite is not very well).

Cassell Bromich Wair the airadrowm wunce wuz.

Chemslee Wud Wair you cud wunce pick blewbells.

Cowsul Wair thairs anutha big ill an yow can see Ams Awl Powa Stay Shun.

Gravly Ill	Fimed for its Spug Etty Junk Shun.
Ilesowin	Wair they mek the chines.
I Mills	Wair they mek the woyer.
Lung Bridge	Wair they mek the Metrows (Wen they int on stroik)
Noo Strate Stay Shun	Diparcha point for Inta-City an the Deesuls.
Sow-ow	See Anns Wuth.
Small Athe	Oam ov the B Essay wair they yewsta mek mowta boiks an guns an awlso oam ov the Blooze.
Solly Ull	Some peepul oo live ere don't loik to be clowsly assowsheatid with Brummies. Oidernow woi. Praps its the wie we tork.
Toislee	A Rile Wie Stay Shun wair yow can still see some owld stame injins.
Wess Bromich	Oam ov Emmanbees Broory an the Albeun oov awsow wun the cup a few toims.
Winsun Grane	Wair the Nick is.
Wulveramtun	Oam ov the One Dras.
	(Yow will nowt oi av incloodid a few plaizis outsoid Brum as well but oi downt spose they'll moind.)

A Dip into Doomsday

(or 1085 an' awl that)

Yow can just imagine worrit wuz loik back in 1085 or thereabouts. There they were — Richard (of Bremingeham — later Brumijum) an' these foiv villeins an' four bordas awl moindin' their own biznis when alung cum these Doomsday blowks, powkin' their nowsis into every other body's biznis. Govamint intaference in rejunal mattas startid lung before ever Parlimint itself woz set up.

Don't be dumb — gew to Brum

It meksya wunda wot they thort, these 'ard wairkin' Brummies as King William's men appeared upon the scene. After awl they 'adn't even got "The Owld Crown" to gew to in those far off days to discuss it over a quick pointer mead. Praps they awl gathered on the banks of the Ray (Rea) an' drowned their sorras in a quick slug of riva worta.

Meanwoil there's these Doomsday blowks walkin' up an' down measurin' the strips an' countin' the oxen an' the plows an' gettin' por owl Richard rather concairned. Acawss it woz awl roit for im really up there in is Manna Rowse. Afta awl 'e woz a mite of William's. Yow can just imagine the last toim they met.

"Yow get yawself a noice little place on that Riva Ray there Richard. Yow neva know wot it moit lead to. Get a few villeins an' serfs around you. Call 'em . . er . . 'Brummies'. That moit start a trend — 'Don't be dumb — gew ter Brum' or 'Mek yaw um in Brum-i-jum' " (that's when the name woz changed — Yow can just imagine William 'avin' a flair for the advertising gimmick).

Sow afta a little debite about the subjict, Richard (now of Brumijum) sets off for the banks of the Ray an' builds is Manna Rowse (or rather 'is serfs do) an' sets up 'is foiv villeins an' four bordas an' awl, an' thinks to 'imself "It's a good way away frum William anyway — Oim not loikly to be bothad boi 'im for awoil".

'An acawss 'is villeins an' bordas flog their guts out for 'im providin' 'im with awl the necessary food woil 'e sits in 'is barownial awl stuffin' 'is 'odge an' knockin' back the occasional cup.

Wot's gewin on in the Woods!?

An' sow loif guz placidly on until this rewral existence is rewdly interruptid by Willaim's blastid civil sairvants oov cum to count the villeins an' measure the arable 'an foind a wood arffa moil lung an' two fairlungs broad (Yow can imagine the "Anglo-Saxon Attitudes" bein' struck in there!). An' afta awl this pacin' up an' roitin' down, Richard asks 'em point blank loik, "Well worrabout it?"

Ownly a Quid's wairth!

"Well," sez the chief scroib, "Oi'll be straight with ya. It woz an' is wairth twenty shillin's"

"Twenty shillin's", sez Richard, tossin' one of 'is owld an' no longer usable serfs on the doyin' foyer, "One measly quid for this lot! Yow muss be outov yaw moind. Down't yow realoise the potential development 'ere? Woi — in a few undrid yairs toim this place will be abserlutely aloiv with Brummies!"

"Ah," sez the scroib, powkin' the simmerin' serf with 'is staff, "Ow can yow be sure of that?"

"Wot the 'ell dya think guz on in the wood arffa moil lung an' two fairlungs broad?" snaps back Richard. "They're a viroil lot these Brummies yu now!"

An' acawss, sroit thou intit?

"Yow'd think boi now it woz time the rest ov the Wairld spowk roit loik us, wudden cha?"

Brumodes, Brumverse and Brumericks

A Lament on the Disparagement of Brumslang

Reflecting on the state of being Brummie,
One remembers that one's oft considered crummy.

Not so with a Geordie or a Scouse,
Whose accents glorified in every house,
Since Beatlemania and "Bonnie Lad"
Became the middle class's latest fad
— Gave them a certain posh renown.

So now it seems that every town,
But Brum, has some mystic feeling
That makes it magic'lly appealing.

Pity the poor disparaged Brummy
Once far-famed for being so chummy!

Now, it seems, the bottom of the heap.
It's enough to make a native weep.
And what's the reason for this misery?

It's plain! — He hasn't had a series on T.V.!

When you consider all the accents rare
And common, which they've put out "on the air"
Since Dixon's Cockney "Evnin' All",
Through "Z-Cars" Lancastrian drawl;

Then "Softly Softly Task Force" here
Brought a touch of Gloucestershire.

Pam Ayres, with her Cotswold Burr,
Made the world aware of her
"Li'ull pomes" as she read them:
Through the country air she led them

John and Ringo, George and Paul
Held the populace in thrall.
Made it known in every house —
How marvellous to be a Scouse!

Then countless groups from Merseyside
Jumped aboard, just for the ride.

Soon we learned — 'twas voiced abroad —
Newcastle's in — you ask Jack Ford!
Then "Bonny Lad" and "Bonny Lass"
Was on the lips of every class.
No-one now thought it was bawdy
To imitate the classic Geordie.

Alf Garnett's Cockney bigotry.
Plain for all the world to see,
Dominated all our screens,
With glo'll stops in all the scenes.

Then Sellers, Emery and Yarwood
And every imitating star would
Take a host of famous persons —
Good 'uns, bad 'uns — even worse 'uns;
Versatility became the gimmick
Of every great and mini-mimic.

Jocks and Taffies, Paddies too,
Chink and Froggy, Gerry and Jew,
Aussies, Yanks and stroppy Boers,
Dutch and Dane and Virile Norse —
When you felt that you had had enough,

After-dinner urbane Ustinov
Joins in the vocif'rous medley,
Tones of Russia issuing readily
From his cosy rotund voice —
Plus much more — you takes your choice —
He'll do you a Bronx New Yorker,
Ambassador or market hawker!
Every tone, nuance and sound
On the airways can be found —

Save for one — O Dear — Cor Lummee!
Where's my lovely native Brummie!

Doan yow reckon now ar kid
It's toim the Brummie med a bid?
Purrar fymous dulcit townes
On the air (an' on the phownes)?
Toim ter gew and tip the balance —
Show the wairld ar nytive talents —
Demonstrite with clarity
As ar townes lack vulgarity —
Toim ter floi the flag for Brum
Toim ter mekya selfa tum
In the corridas of fime —
Toim ter mekya selfa nime?

P.S. Though — I'd strike a medal
For Miss Reid — I mean our Beryl
With her delectable Marlene,
Plus a gong for Don Maclean.

And finally — well Jasper Carratt — he
Can intone with Brummie clarity.
So perhaps there's still a chance
For our Brummie elegance
To be dragged from where it's gone
Right back to Division One.

Brumericks

Wot meks a Brummy so chummy?
Cor Lummee — it must be is mummy
    Or in later years
    The assortment of beers
Wot e pours every noit down is tummy.

A cairly young gairly from Shairley
Wore short skirts that were terribly twairly
    When she bent to her shoe
    She revealed a view
That sent most randy men in a whairly.

There was a young fellow from Mowslee
Planned a noit with is girl friend quite cowslee
    She thought "This might be tricky"
    And slipped him a micky
And he ended performing quite dowslee.

A nubile young lady from Witton
Had a face like a Siamese kitten
    She had whiskers as well
    So it's easy to tell
Why the fellas weren't easily smitten.

An Asian once living in Aston
Refrained from all food with the fast on.
    And throughout Ramadhan
    So complete was his plan
That the poor fellow faded and passed on.

A fellow who lived in Great Barr,
On the golf course was quite under par.
   He was lazy "an' awl"
   So he gave up the crawl
And went round the links in his car.

An ardent musician of Sandwell
Was determined to tutor his band well
   So down at the pub
   He fed 'em some grub
And soon they were certainly "canned" well.

But booze and rehearsals don't mix
So he found he was in quite a fix.
   He sobered 'em up
   With coffee to sup
And made 'em play on until six.

Soon he found the expense was no joke,
What with coffee and grub and rum coke.
   This fellow from Sandwell
   Can now understand well
That feting your band makes you broke.
— Just stick to the notes and you're Oke!

A Little More Serious
(and Nostalgic)
Verse

Maggoty Brook

As a boy I recall being taken by my older sister and her friends on many Sunday afternoon walks to a place in the vicinity of Buckland's End Lane called "Maggoty Brook". I don't know who thought of this Dickensian name but I remember well what it was like.

"Come for a walk," my sister said
And led me with her friend
Down country lanes so near
The city that they smelled
Of sewerage in the ditch.

"Come for a walk down Maggoty Brook
Where the frogspawn lies in clusters
Thick enough to ladle
Into jam jars for your nature class.
Walk for a while (but don't tell Dad
That I'm meeting a boy at the end of the lane
By Maggoty Brook)".

Maggoty Brook's a smelly stream
Dying of factory poison.
Maggoty Brook's a laddy's dream
When tadpole are in season.

Maggoty Brook is muddy and dark —
Dare you to put your feet in.
Newts in the water, rats on the bank
And tiddlers always fleeting.

They say if you throw a match in
And let it float all free,
It'll drift to the Tame and then to the Trent
And one day reach the sea.

And under the trees there are monsters
And cowboys and Indians too
And cannibals in the jungle
And Long John Silver's crew.

You've only to close your eyes there
When you've read your explorer's book
And you'll hear the roar of the Amazon
From the babble of Maggoty Brook.

"Time to go," my sister said,
"And don't you tell our Dad!
Here's a penny for some chocolate".
    I think they've all gone mad!

Stechford Station

I was appalled to see one day some years ago that they were removing the familiar wooden entrance to Stechford Station, a place which had been my springing off point for dozens of childhood journeys, as well as a train-spotting centre. Only real railway enthusiasts will feel the nostalgia in this poem.

They're tearing Stechford Station down, I see —
Yet more of British Rail's economy.
Now every little boy, near middle age,
Will sigh a little for his heritage.

For days of "Joobs" and "Baby Scots" and all
The splendour of "The Irish Mail's" call.
The earthquake on the platform as she tore
The place asunder touching eighty four.

And "Standard Compounds, "Claughtons", "Royal Scots",
Tankers, "O-Six-O's" and "Patriots"
Will puffer through the outposts of the mind —
Ticked off in little books of every kind.

"There's something "pegged" back there along the track!"
A distant puff of smoke is seen way back —
Anticipation wells. What will it be?
A scruffy tanker or . . . "The Silver Jubilee"!

The platform's still once more. The shunting tank
Intrudes with noisy steam and idle clank
On to the main line — just to switch a load —
Then hastily retreats to clear the road.

Well — It's all electric now and diesel fumes.
Empty seats and lonely waiting rooms.
They're tearing Stechford Station down I see.
No more "copping" trains for you and me.

Yardley Cemetery

(In their sad loss)

Death always seemed a much gloomier affair when I was a child
than it does now and I could rarely understand exactly what people
had died of. My parents and aunts always took me along on their
graveside tidying pilgrimages. I never understood what it was all
about, really. Perhaps one never does.

Here beneath the carven crosses, sculpted books,
Marble chippings, "Taken from us" quotes,
Fading flowers, bird-faeced tombstones,
Lies my older generation.
Edwardo-Victoriana, brass-bedsteaded
Aunts and uncles from "respectable" homes.

        Alf, who died of pilchard poison in the hospital
        After falling off his sit-up-begging bicycle
        And breaking his leg.

        Edith, whom the sudden stroke took off.
        Nell, who read her virginity to death.
        Gentle consumptive Walter of fourteen years.
        Herbert, the nut and bolt tycoon.
        Edwin — the flop.

All these had proper funerals, oaken coffins,
Floral send-offs, real priests,
Black-bordered cards on wreaths . . .

        . . . "In Loving Memory" . . .
        And the "notice" in the "*Mail*"

And tears on the cheeks of the mourners
Splashing into the open grave
And ham and tea for "afters".

As a child, I trailed with mother and aunt,
Puzzled by this ritual jaunt,
Bunched flowers, discreetly chosen,
Tired feet and fingers frozen,
Up the asphalt pathway, straight
Up to the tombstone near the gate,
Ceremonially silent, voices still —
A dozen big chrysanths for Uncle Bill,
A Christmas wreath for Aunty Nell.
And, in the air the corpses' smell
Arising from the carven crosses.
From the family's sad losses.

Castle Bromwich Aerodrome

(Empire Day)

There was a great romantic aura surrounding Castle Bromwich Aerodrome before the war. It seemed a great pity when it was neglected after 1945. I suppose the best thing that could have happened in the present situation, is that it should have been made into a housing estate. Perhaps that's what the men in the poem would have preferred, in which case the word "splendid" might well replace "squalid" in the last line but one. But I'm sure there will be some romantics who will know what I mean by "squalid".

Here, where concrete boxes stand erect,
"Reach-for-the-Sky" men once in barracks slept.
And hangars housed the silver streamlined planes —
"Hart" and "Hind" and "Fury". Magic names
To fascinate and challenge little boys
To fly above the clouds with manly poise —

To spin and roll and weave and turn and bank —
Dip wings at shoulder height along the flank
Of watching crowds — held breathless for a spell
As power-diving "Angels-out-of-Hell"
Prepared themselves for battle yet to be
And nineteen forty's moral victory.

How squalid that this pioneering trail
Be turned to blocks of flats like Castle Vale.

The Bull Ring

Standing in the new Bull Ring Centre one day, my mind turned back to the old cobbled street always packed with people and little girls and boys crushed in the crowds.

Beneath the Schweppe's sign's effervescent dwindle,
Where the red bull snorts.
Near the curving sidewalk's spindle,
By the market courts.
Where the angry traffic vaults the subway —
Grubby concrete even now.

By the posh new stalls at mid-day,
There stands a ghost stall
Selling soft tomatoes;
And a Saturday crush
Suffocating little children
Mingling with the crawling cars
Climbing the cobbled hill
By the Market Hall.

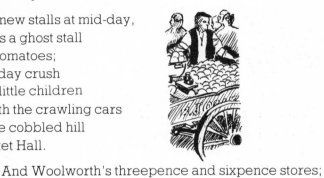

And Woolworth's threepence and sixpence stores;
Centre of penny leaden soldiers
And tinsel for Christmas time
And greasy peanuts in tupenny bags
And cheap and nasty chocolate
Men with magic cases
Full of tatty Eastern toys
Sicking drunken men and grubby boys
And always, underfoot, squashy dirt and litter
And my head crushed between bloomered thighs
Clutching my new Dinky Toy.

Frankley Beeches

There is one place near the Frankley Reservoir where the water gushes forth at the end of its long journey from the Elan Valley. It seems we in Birmingham take our excellent water supply very much for granted without considering the sacrifices that have been made to get it to us.

Out past the city suburbs lie the lakes
Which slake the city's thirsty industry —
Vast man-made bowls beneath the trees
Of Frankley. With civilised facility
We turn a tap and taste the easy flow
And make our tea and wash our paths and cars,
Refresh our lawns and gossip in our bars
And grumble when the world lies thick with snow.

And here from the earth — from one small hole,
Roars water from the Elan Reservoirs.
And in the flood is the sound of the soul
Of sunken farms and homes and villages,
Displaced persons, drowning cows and sheep,
Glutted crops and fields and trees — asleep.

Widow in Aston

There have been many instances of old inhabitants refusing to leave their houses before being bulldozed for redevelopment.

I shall not move from this house,
Where my children were born,
To make way for a slick new motorway
Or a polished office block,
Or a tower of flats for newly-weds
Six hundred council beds into the sky.

I shall not leave my little terraced room
With the vandal-smashed windows
And the "Go-home Pakis" paintings
On the wall —
Just for the sake of officialdom.

I shall stay here in my own invented grime —
Good, clean, happy-families, sibling-sifted muck
On my only-lonely own —
Desperate for sympathy
But unbowed
Before the bulldozer.

Immigrants on a Rainy Night

I do not think that this poem needs any explanation.

It is raining tonight.
It is raining in Balsall Heath
And, therefore, in Barbados
And Pakistan.
It is raining in the Punjab
And Jamaica.

It is wet in St. Kitts.
Cyprus is wet.
It is raining in Indian homes
And Kenyan compounds.

It is lashing the world, brothers and sisters,
But it will not wash the blue from my eye
Or the black from your skin.
It will not wash you out
Or wash me in.

It is raining on the bodies of Buchenwald
And in Flanders and Arnhem.
Even the wigwams are leaking
And the igloos.
And Chairman Mao gets wet when it is raining
Like Mohammed did
And Jesus . . . wept.

All over town tonight, it is raining.